Healthy Lifestyles

DEALING WITH DRUGS

Anne Rooney

amicus
mankato, minnesota

This book has been published in cooperation with Evans Publishing Group.

© Evans Brothers Limited 2010
This edition published under license from Evans Brothers Limited.

Published in the United States by
Amicus
P.O. Box 1329, Mankato, Minnesota 56002

Printed in China by Midas Printing International Ltd

Anne Rooney has asserted her moral right to be recognized as the author of this work.

Consultant: Adrian King
Editor: Sonya Newland
Designer: Graham Rich
Picture researcher: Sophie Schrey

Library of Congress Cataloging-in-Publication Data

Rooney, Anne.
  Dealing with drugs / Anne Rooney.
    p. cm. -- (Healthy lifestyles)
  Summary: "Discusses the risks and realities of teenage drug use and abuse, including alcohol, marijuana, tobacco, prescription drugs, steroids, inhalants, party drugs such as ecstasy, and more." -- Provided by publisher
  Includes index.
  ISBN 978-1-60753-084-8 (lib. bdg.)
  1. Drugs--Juvenile literature. 2. Drugs--Physiological effect--Juvenile literature. I. Title.
  RM301.17.R66 2011
  615'.1--dc22

                    2009047570

Picture Credits
Alamy: cover (Janine Wiedel Photolibrary), 9 (Angela Hampton Picture Library), 11l (Angela Hampton Picture Library), 18 (David Hoffman Photo Library), cover b and 25 (David Hoffman Photo Library), 30 (David Hoffman Photo Library), 31 (Mark Harvey), 37 (TravelStockCollection - Homer Sykes), 38 (Janine Wiedel Photolibrary), 41 (David Hoffman Photo Library); **Corbis:** 6 (Atlantide Phototravel), 7 (David Vintiner), 16 (SGO/Image Point FR), 29t (Olivier Prevosto/TempSport), 32 (Jennie Woodcock/Reflections Photolibrary), 35t (Scott Houston/Sygma), 36 (Floris Leeuwenberg/The Cover Story), 40 (Reuters), 42 (Scott Houston); **Fotolia:** 15b (Fotolia VI), 28 (Smalik); **Getty Images:** 13r (WireImage), 15t, 26; **iStock:** 10 (Bob Thomas), 11r (Alain Juteau), 12 (Don Wilkie), 13l (Webphotographer), 19 (Diego Cervo), 20 (Diane White Rosier), 22l (Karen Phillips), 22r (Sean Locke), 23 (Joselito Briones), 27 (Charles Taylor), 33 (Paul Kline), 34 (Levi Webb), cover tr and 39 (Nick Stone), 43 (Mike Cherim); **Science Photo Library:** 17 (A. Glauberman), 24 (Mark Thomas); **Shutterstock:** 8 (Monkey Business Images), 14 (Elliott Westacott), 21 (Frances A. Miller), 29b (Damir Karan), cover m and 35b (Gregor Kervina).
Artwork by Graham Rich

05 10
PO 1560

9 8 7 6 5 4 3 2 1

Contents

Introduction

There are many messages about the use and misuse of drugs. Understanding the facts about drugs can help you make the right decisions and stay healthy.

You might not realize it, but coffee contains a drug—caffeine—that can change your mood.

Are All Drugs Harmful?

A drug is anything that affects the way your mind or body works. That includes medicines, legal substances such as alcohol and cigarettes, and illegal street drugs. Some people rely on drugs prescribed by their doctors in order to stay healthy. Many more occasionally use over-the-counter (OTC) medicines to deal with minor complaints such as headaches or hay fever. These medicines are drugs, but used sensibly and safely they cause no harm and often make life more comfortable for people. But drugs can be harmful if they are wrongly used.

There are many mood-altering chemicals in things we eat and drink. Caffeine, for example, is a mood-altering chemical found in coffee and tea. In moderation, this is usually harmless. Legal drugs include alcohol and tobacco. Many adults drink moderate amounts of alcohol with no harm.

DID YOU KNOW?

Among the most addictive drugs are nicotine, crystal methamphetamine, and Valium (diazepam). Nicotine is legal, as is Valium with a prescription. Crystal meth is illegal.

Indeed, research suggests that small amounts of alcohol may even be good for adults, but too much alcohol or caffeine can be damaging.

Drugs that are sold illegally are generally considered to be more harmful. It is true that drugs such as skunk (strong marijuana) and heroin can have devastating effects on people's lives—but so can the legal drug nicotine. The legal status of a substance is not always a good indicator of how safe it is.

Most people can enjoy alcohol in moderation without feeling like they need it, but some can become psychologically dependendent on it.

Addiction and Dependency

Some drugs can be habit forming, which means people feel compelled to keep taking them.

Sometimes, people become psychologically dependent on a drug: they feel that they must have it to function normally or to stay happy. It can be very difficult to stop using the drug.

Other drugs cause physical dependency (addiction). An addict may suffer physical side effects if they stop taking the drug. Many substances can cause addiction, including legal, illegal, and prescription drugs—it is possible to become addicted to some medical (prescribed) drugs, too. Not everyone who uses an addictive drug becomes addicted. Some people are more prone to becoming dependent on drugs than others. A lot depends on the individual and his or her circumstance.

FEEL-GOOD FACTOR

If you are worried about your use of any substance—legal or illegal—you can get confidential advice and help from a medical professional, a drug counseling service, or student-support staff at your school. Asking for advice can put your mind at rest or help you stop taking a drug.

Alcohol

Alcohol is the most widely used drug in modern society. Many adults drink sometimes, and most enjoy a few drinks safely, but too much alcohol can harm a person's body.

Why Do People Drink?

Most people who drink do so because they like the taste of alcoholic drinks or the way alcohol makes them feel. Drinking is usually a social activity: people drink with their friends when they are having fun. Alcohol helps people to lose their inhibitions. They relax and become less self-conscious or less nervous. This can be a good feeling, but it can lead to problems, too. Sometimes people take foolish risks or say or do things they regret later. If you feel drunk, it means your body is not able to deal with the amount of alcohol you have consumed.

Many young people drink alcohol on a night out because it helps them relax and enjoy themselves.

What Do Young People Drink?

Many young people drink beer because it is often cheaper than other alcoholic drinks. If they want to get drunk but they don't want to consume a large volume of liquid, they might drink hard alcohol, such as vodka. Alcohol is usually mixed with nonalcoholic drinks such as fruit juice or soft drinks to make them taste better. It can be easy to lose track of how much alcohol you've consumed when drinking like this or when drinking sweet alcoholic drinks, because they don't taste very strong.

At parties, people sometimes make mixed alcoholic drinks such as punch. Unless you made it yourself, you won't know how much or what types of alcohol is in it. Also, people may add alcohol to the punch throughout the evening, so it might be stronger than you realize. In these situations, it's always safest to stick to drinks you can pour yourself from a bottle or can.

DID YOU KNOW?

Watching TV shows and advertisements that feature alcohol encourages people to drink more. A study in 2009 found that young people drank twice as much during an evening's viewing if the program or commercials showed people drinking alcohol.

Safe Drinking

Useful guidelines indicate how much adults can safely drink without usually harming their bodies. It is based on what the adult body can metabolize. One alcoholic drink is 12 ounces of beer, 5 ounces of wine, or 1.5 ounces of distilled spirits such as vodka. For those who are not on medication, the suggested daily limit is two drinks for men and one drink for women. Drinking less than the maximum is better than drinking up to the limit every week, but even within the safe limits, it can be dangerous to drink it all in just a few sessions. It's best to have one or more alcohol-free days each week. And don't drink and drive!

Young people cannot safely drink as much as adults. Their bodies are not fully developed and the liver is not yet able to process alcohol well. The legal age to drink is 21 in the United States and varies from 18 to 19 in Canada. The National Institutes of Health recommends people under 21 should not drink alcohol at all.

Some soft drinks or fruit juices are premixed with alcohol. These drinks often do not taste very alcoholic, and it can be difficult to be aware of how much alcohol you have consumed.

REAL LIFE

"I didn't drink because, as a Muslim, I'm not allowed. It got boring looking after everyone at parties. Plus, there's that sense of curiosity. I wondered what it felt like. I decided to try it, but maybe because I wasn't used to it I thought it tasted horrible!" Mehreen, 18

WHAT'S IN IT?

Sometimes people "spike" other people's drinks—they add extra alcohol or sometimes a drug. To make sure you know what's in your drink, order your own, and never leave your drink unattended. You can purchase special cards or coasters with chemical patches on them. If you put a drop of your drink on the patch and it changes color, someone has spiked your drink with a drug.

Alcohol

People may drink because they don't want to feel left out during parties or celebrations—they think it's no fun being the only sober one.

Mix and Match

Mixing drinks and other drugs can be much more dangerous than just drinking alcohol. Sometimes the effects of alcohol on the body mean that other drugs will have a greater effect than they would on their own. This applies to all drugs, including prescription and over-the-counter medicines, and even herbal remedies. If you take medicines, look at the product information or ask your doctor whether it is safe to drink alcohol when you are taking them. You should never take acetaminophen or aspirin if you are drinking.

FEEL-GOOD FACTOR

Peer pressure can be difficult. If you will be with other teens who drink, plan ahead on how to say no to drinking. Or try these ways to say no:
No thanks!
I'd rather have a soda.
I'm having fun without drinking.
I have to be up early in the morning.

"Everyone Does It"

Some young people say they drink because their friends drink and they want to be part of the crowd. They want to have fun when they're out socially and don't want to be the only sober one when everyone else is drinking. But not everyone drinks. Some people don't drink because their religion prohibits it. Some don't like the flavor of alcohol or the feeling of being drunk and out of control. Some people don't drink for health reasons. In many countries, it is illegal for people under a certain age to buy alcohol or drink it in public; respect for or fear of the law discourages some people.

Joining In

No one should drink just because other people want them to. If you feel under pressure, remember that your feeling that other people want you to drink may well be more powerful than their real desire for you to join them. They might encourage you to join in, but they are unlikely to be bothered if you choose not to. Show that you are mature enough to make your own choices by taking responsibility for what you opt to do. If your friends put a lot of pressure on you to do something you don't want to do, consider whether or not they are really friends.

If friends make you feel bad about not drinking or bully you into it, then they're not really friends at all.

Alcohol's Effect on the Body

When you drink alcohol, a little of it (about 10 percent) is broken down in the stomach. The rest is absorbed through the wall of the stomach into the bloodstream. Some is quickly removed in the liver, but the rest circulates and affects other parts of the body. It is slowly removed as the blood passes through the liver again and again. Alcohol can damage the tissues of the body, particularly the liver and the brain. People who drink a lot of alcohol over an extended period can develop such serious liver disease that they need a liver transplant in order to survive.

Women's tolerance for alcohol is lower than men's. Its effects can occur more quickly. You may be sick or even pass out from drinking too much.

SAFE LIMITS

Alcohol is not absorbed by fat cells. Women tend to have a higher proportion of body fat than men, so alcohol is concentrated into a smaller proportion of their body and has a greater effect than it would on a man. This is why the recommended safe limit is lower for women than for men.

Alcohol

Overdoing It

Many people who are alcohol-dependent drink every day, often in large quantities. Alcoholics may feel they cannot face the day without drinking, but not all people dependent on alcohol fit this pattern. There are many people who regularly drink more than the guidelines suggest and would not consider that they have a problem with alcohol.

Thousands of people around the world are killed every year in car accidents related to alcohol use.

Some young people do not drink much or at all during the week but drink a great deal on weekends. Drinking a lot in one session is known as "binge drinking." It places great stress on the body, which suddenly has to deal with more alcohol in a single session than it can safely handle in a week. It is much more harmful to drink 10 or 20 units in a single night than spread over a week. Extreme binge drinking is very dangerous and can lead to alcohol poisoning. This can be fatal or cause permanent brain damage.

Not Just the Drink

Alcohol is a depressant drug, which means that it slows your reaction time as well as affecting your coordination and judgment. After drinking too much, people are more likely to make mistakes, do something dangerous, or have an accident. If you are drunk, you may make ill-judged choices (such as committing a crime or having unprotected sex), try dangerous tricks, or just fall and hurt yourself. Alcohol and drugs are involved in many road accidents.

Alcohol Use and Misuse

Many people experiment with drugs for a while and then stop. People who try alcohol as children often dislike it, but they may start drinking again when they get older. They may continue to drink and perhaps start taking other drugs. Their use might be casual, recreational, or even regular without becoming addictive. Casual use is occasional use. A casual drinker does not mind whether they drink or not. Many people are casual drinkers, having an occasional glass of wine or beer. Recreational use involves taking a drug as part of having a good time, often with other people. Drinking is often recreational, as people do it with their friends and at social events. Regular use means using the drug on a regular basis, perhaps even most days. Some people develop patterns or habits in their lives in which alcohol is a regular feature—having a drink after work, for example.

DID YOU KNOW?

Two people who share a bottle of wine with dinner every night and drink no other alcohol, each drink 32 units a week—that's well over the recommended limit for both men and women.

Casual use is when people drink occasionally with friends. Casual drinkers can take it or leave it and do not feel a need to drink.

British Pop star Amy Winehouse has well-publicized problems with both alcohol and drugs. It can take time before some people even realize they have a problem.

A Drinking Problem?

Drug use becomes misuse when it interferes with a person's life or with their physical or mental well-being. Their drug use may be chaotic or dependent, disrupting their normal functioning and causing problems. Sometimes people are not aware that their drug use has become a problem and turned into misuse; they may believe that they still have it under control. It can be easy to ignore a problem with a legal and socially acceptable drug such as alcohol, because people can use it openly and obtain it easily. Some people who drink enough to harm their health do not recognize they have a problem.

REAL LIFE

"The week before our wedding, my fiancé went on a stag night with some of his friends. The next morning, his father was on my doorstep in tears. Craig had died of alcohol poisoning a few hours before. I can't begin to describe how I felt. It has wrecked my life."
Georgia, 26

Tobacco

Many young people try cigarettes just to see what smoking is like, but some go on to become regular smokers. Once you start smoking, it can be difficult to stop.

In the past, cigarette companies raised their profile by sponsoring sporting events such as Formula One racing. This occurs less often as many countries have now banned cigarette advertising at Grand Prix events.

Why Start Smoking?

For many people, trying smoking is an adventure—they are curious and want to experiment. Perhaps there are others in their household who smoke, so trying cigarettes seems natural. Sometimes parents who are smokers send the wrong message by saying a young person is "not old enough to smoke." This suggests that smoking is a grown-up thing to do and makes it more attractive. It also suggests that there is a time when smoking is appropriate.

Older movies often show smoking as glamorous, and the sponsorship of sports events by tobacco companies sends out a message that tobacco is cool. Research published in 2007 showed that young people in Germany exposed to films that showed smoking were more than twice as likely to smoke as those who did not view such films. It is hardly surprising that young people try tobacco when they are bombarded by images that make it look cool and sexy.

Worldwide, about one in five teens smokes. Nine out of ten adult U.S. smokers began smoking as teenagers.

NICOTINE ADDICTION

The drug in tobacco, nicotine, is the most addictive drug known. Giving up smoking can be harder than giving up illegal street drugs such as crack cocaine and heroin. If tobacco were only just discovered now, it would probably be illegal in most countries.

Around half of teenage smokers continue to smoke for at least 15 years. Half of those who continue to smoke as adults will die of smoking-related conditions. On average, each cigarette shortens a person's life expectancy by five minutes—about the length of time it takes to smoke it.

Between 80,000 and 100,000 young people take up smoking every day—half of them in Asia.

Smoking and the Law

In many countries, it is illegal for children and young people to buy tobacco, and smoking is illegal in many enclosed public places. In the United States it is illegal to sell tobacco to anyone under 18. Even though it is more difficult for teens to buy cigarettes, more than 150 million packs are sold to teens annually. The number of young smokers is not decreasing. This pattern is the same all over the world.

DID YOU KNOW?

One person dies from a smoking-related illness every 6.5 seconds around the world. Someone who starts smoking as a teenager and continues for 20 years is likely to die 20 to 25 years earlier than a nonsmoker.

The Dangers of Smoking

Smoking can lead to many kinds of illness. Smokers have an increased risk of lung cancer and other types of cancer including cancer of the mouth, cervix, throat, bladder, and kidneys. Smokers are also more likely to suffer from breathing difficulties and lung conditions such as bronchitis, emphysema, and asthma, and from heart disease and stroke.

Living with Smokers

Many young smokers are first exposed to smoking at home. Exposure to tobacco smoke is harmful even for someone who does not smoke. This is called secondhand smoking. Children who live with smokers are more likely to take up smoking than those who live in nonsmoking households. Research shows that even if they don't smoke themselves, young people who live with smokers have a 20–30 percent higher risk of lung cancer than people who don't live with smokers. People who regularly breathe secondhand smoke also have less efficient brains and perform less well in tests of mental ability.

Children who grow up around parents who smoke are at much higher risk of some diseases. They are also more likely to become smokers.

Tobacco

There are many options to help you quit smoking, including chewing gum, nicotine patches, and pills. Your doctor can help you decide which is best for you.

Giving Up

Many smokers decide to quit. It can be difficult to do. But with enough willpower and support, it is possible. Some young people quit because they realize the damage that smoking is doing to their health. Others give up because smoking is very expensive and they want to spend the money on more lasting items or on enjoying themselves in other ways. If you were to smoke 10 cigarettes a day from the age of 15 to the age of 80, it would cost you more than $82,000 in today's money.

FEEL-GOOD FACTOR

If you are trying to quit smoking, remind yourself that, besides the health benefits, there are financial ones, too! Every time you would buy a pack of cigarettes, put the money in a jar. You'll soon see how quickly it adds up. When you have quit for a month, use the money to buy something nice for yourself.

Looking Good

Most nonsmokers find the smell of smoke unpleasant. Some young people give up smoking because they have boyfriends or girlfriends who do not smoke. Smoking has a big impact on physical appearance, too. Apart from stained fingers and teeth, it leads to poor skin that grays and wrinkles at a young age.

Reversing the Damage

It takes just six seconds for the nicotine in cigarette smoke to reach your brain. Within 20 seconds of stopping, your body starts to recover. Your heart rate and blood pressure drop back to normal. Within hours, the levels of carbon monoxide in the blood starts to drop. Within weeks of quitting, your circulation will improve, you won't produce as much phlegm, and you will cough and wheeze less. Within a few months, lung function improves considerably.

In the long term, quitting reduces the chances of cancer, heart disease, and other illnesses caused by smoking. Those who give up smoking at age 30 reduce their chances of dying of a smoking-related disease by 90 percent (although it is never as low as for a person who has never smoked).

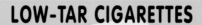

LOW-TAR CIGARETTES

Approximately 4,000 chemicals are in cigarette smoke, of which at least 250 are harmful and 50 can cause cancer. Cigarettes also produce a thick, yellowish-brown tar that builds up in the lungs and stains smokers' teeth and fingers. So-called low-tar or ultra low-tar cigarettes are no less harmful than any others and carry the same risks of lung cancer.

Side Effects of Quitting

Some people find giving up smoking more difficult than others, but it is always easier to give up sooner rather than later. If your body has become physically dependent on nicotine, you might feel anxious, depressed, sad, restless, or have difficulty sleeping—this is quite normal and will pass. You may gain weight, but you are unlikely to gain very much.

Getting Help

There is plenty of help available if you want to give up smoking. Many people use aids such as nicotine patches, lozenges, or gum, which provide a measured dose of nicotine to the body. These help you deal with nicotine cravings while you break the habit and become accustomed to not having a cigarette in your hand. Some people find that they miss the routine of smoking. It can be easier to tackle this first and wean yourself off the nicotine afterward by reducing your use of patches or gum. There is no known harmful effect of using nicotine replacement products, even for a long time.

A healthy lung (left) is compared to a smoker's lung. The smoker's lung is darker, rougher, and misshapen. Nicotine and tar can cause cancerous tumors that destroy the lung tissue.

Marijuana

Marijuana is the most widely used illegal drug in the world. Although some people argue that compared to drinking too much alcohol or smoking cigarettes, the risks associated with marijuana are relatively small. But long-term heavy use of marijuana can have devastating effects.

Smoking, Eating, and Drinking

Marijuana is a drug made from the marijuana plant and is available as leaf or resin (a solid plant substance). As a leaf, it is rolled into thin cigarettes, called joints, and smoked. Many people roll it with tobacco, but it can also be smoked in a pipe, or cooked and eaten in food. "Hash brownies" are brownies that contain marijuana. Marijuana can be dissolved in milk, and some people take it in coffee.

The leaves of the marijuana plant can be dried and rolled up with tobacco to be smoked as a joint. It is also available as a resin.

you or want to hurt you. It can make you giggle at the slightest things. It can also make you very hungry so that you eat a lot, including unhealthy food, which can result in weight gain. Some people feel sick after smoking marijuana and some have panic attacks. These are frightening episodes when your heart races and you feel as if you can't breathe.

Marijuana is available in different forms and different strengths, but all carry risks. In particular, the powerful form "skunk" can cause mental illnesses such as depression and schizophrenia in a small number of users.

Effects of Marijuana

Marijuana is a mild sedative, which means it can make you feel relaxed, talkative, and happy. It can have a hallucinogenic effect if used a lot, making you see or imagine things that aren't really there. It can make you feel paranoid—unreasonably scared that people hate

Marijuana can also make any existing mental-health problem worse. If there is a history of mental illness in your family, using marijuana increases your risk of developing mental health problems.

EASING THE PAIN

Some people use marijuana to relieve the pain of a severe medical condition. It is illegal to supply or grow marijuana even for medical use. People who want to use it in this way often accept, reluctantly, that they are breaking the law.

Moving On

You may have heard marijuana described as a gateway drug. This means that people may start using marijuana and move on to other drugs. In fact, most people who misuse drugs begin with legal drugs—tobacco or alcohol—and move on from there. Many experiment with marijuana after smoking cigarettes or drinking and move on to illegal drugs other than marijuana. There is no evidence that people who try marijuana after using tobacco or alcohol are more likely than anyone else to become addicted to other illegal drugs.

Although most people who go on to use other street drugs have used marijuana, most people who use marijuana do not go on to use other illegal drugs.

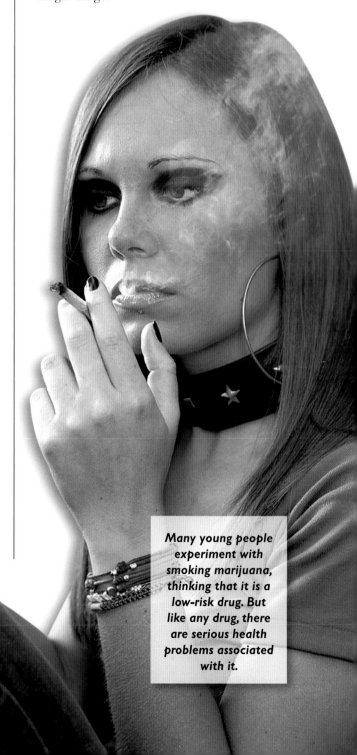

Many young people experiment with smoking marijuana, thinking that it is a low-risk drug. But like any drug, there are serious health problems associated with it.

Marijuana

marijuana takes in three to five times as much tar and carbon monoxide as someone smoking tobacco cigarettes. Generally, tobacco smokers smoke more frequently than people smoking joints, but one joint can have the same harmful effect on the lungs as smoking up to 20 cigarettes. A study in 2008 found that people who smoked one joint a day for 10 years were nearly six times as likely to get lung cancer as those who didn't smoke any.

Taking Care

As with alcohol, there are additional short-term dangers of using marijuana. Because the drug can affect coordination and reaction times, it is not safe to drive or operate machinery after using marijuana. Reaction time is reduced by up to 40 percent after one joint and as

Overuse

Those who use marijuana often may build up resistance to the chemical that produces its impact in the brain, so they don't feel the same effects after using it for a long time. On the other hand, consistent use can leave some people feeling permanently stoned, even when they have not recently used marijuana.

Another Form of Smoking

Many people who use marijuana roll it into a joint with leaf tobacco and may not use filters. Filters prevent some of the harmful chemicals from entering the body. Without filters, the smoker is exposed to the damaging effects of tobacco and marijuana. Someone smoking

EFFECTS OF OVERUSE

Although eating or drinking marijuana avoids the harmful effects associated with smoking the drug, it is easier to take too much if you eat it. It may also make you feel sick or uncomfortable. Overdosing on marijuana can lead to severe panic attacks, dry mouth, and feeling disoriented, delirious, or feverish.

Police dogs are trained to sniff out drugs such as marijuana. They are often used at airports to make sure people aren't smuggling the drug. Dogs are used anywhere police suspect people may have drugs.

much as 60 percent after smoking two joints. If you are going to use marijuana, do so in a safe environment and don't use a bicycle or drive any type of motor vehicle while affected by it.

Giving Up

While marijuana is not physically addictive, if you roll it with tobacco, there is the danger of becoming addicted to nicotine. Some users develop a strong psychological dependency on marijuana that can make it difficult to give up the habit. If you have used marijuana for a long time and stop using it, you may feel anxious, lose your appetite, and find it difficult to sleep.

DID YOU KNOW?

About one in five young people aged 17 and 18 in the United States uses marijuana regularly; half have tried it at least once. About one in three Canadian teenagers say they have tried marijuana at least once.

These effects may start a day after you stop, peak at two to three days, and disappear within a week or two.

If you want to give up or cut down, it can help to keep a record for a few weeks of when you feel like having a joint and when you actually do have one. This will show your pattern of use. You might be able to spot triggers—people or situations that make you more likely to use marijuana. Then you can reduce your exposure to those triggers to help you cut down your use and eventually stop completely.

Medical Drugs

Many people use prescription or over-the-counter medicines on a regular basis in order to keep a medical condition under control or to deal with minor ailments. In most cases, their use is beneficial, but it is possible to misuse medical drugs.

Regulating Medicines

In most countries, a government agency sets rules and standards to control how medicines are made and supplied. This ensures medicines are made safely and tested thoroughly, that they contain only safe ingredients, and do what they are supposed to do with limited side effects. It also ensures that they are available only through properly licensed outlets, such as pharmacists. Some medicines are available only by prescription, so it is not possible to get them legally without a medical doctor or other authorized health practitioner prescribing the drug.

Although medicines are usually carefully controlled, there is still a black market in which they are made or sold illegally. In some cases, it is illegal to possess a medicine if you don't have a prescription for it. The tranquilizer temazepam (a sedative) is one example. In other cases, possession is not illegal. However, supplying the medicine to someone without a prescription is illegal.

Strong medical drugs are carefully controlled and can only be dispensed by doctors and pharmacists.

Some people, such as asthma sufferers, have a long-term health issue that means they may have to take medical drugs on a regular basis.

Long-term and Short-term Drug Use

Some people need to take a medical drug regularly to control a long-term condition. People who suffer from asthma may use inhalers regularly. People with diabetes use a drug called insulin to control their blood sugar levels. People with epilepsy use medication to keep from having seizures. Regular medication can also be used to control mental health problems such as depression or attention deficit hyperactivity disorder (ADHD).

Always carefully read the packaging of any prescription drugs and take them exactly as directed.

DID YOU KNOW?

In 2006, U.S. doctors wrote 1.8 billion drug prescriptions for patients; 71 percent of patients were given drugs after they visited their doctor.

Most people will be prescribed drugs to deal with a medical condition at some time in their lives, whether it is antibiotics for an infection or powerful chemotherapy drugs to treat cancer. Many people buy medicines over the counter to treat minor ailments such as headaches, period pains, allergies, and colds. A few people carry specific drugs to use in an emergency. For example, someone allergic to nuts may carry an EpiPen to give themselves a shot of adrenalin if they accidentally eat nuts. All these drugs, if used safely, improve health, give a better quality of life, or save lives.

Using Medicines Safely

If you have to use a medicine, follow the instructions given by your doctor or on the package. If the instructions say to take the drug with meals, do so—taking a medicine with food changes the rate at which it is absorbed and that may be important in making sure it is effective and safe. If you are given a course of medical drugs, follow the course to the end. You may feel better before the infection is completely cleared from your body, but it can flare up again if you don't finish the course.

REAL LIFE

"I got in an argument with a boy at school and he pushed me against a concrete window ledge, cutting my head. As I have hemophilia, there was blood everywhere—my blood never clots, I just go on bleeding. A teacher got my emergency injection for me; it's a replacement clotting factor, so the bleeding stops."
Jason, 13

Medical Drugs

Mixing Medicines

It is not safe to mix medicines, take medicines with other drugs, or drink alcohol while taking medicines unless your doctor has said that it is all right to do so. Some antibiotics will not work if taken with alcohol. The effect of some drugs may be increased or decreased if taken with alcohol or other drugs. It can be dangerous to take medicines prescribed for someone else or share your prescription medicines. The doctor takes into account each patient's needs, body, and medical history when prescribing a drug, so you may not be given the same medicine as someone else with the same condition.

Enough Is Enough

It can be dangerous to take more than the stated dose of a medicine. If a medicine is not making you feel better, don't assume you can just take more or start taking something else as well. There may be a different medicine that will be better suited to your body and your condition, so contact your doctor or pharmacist for further advice. Always check the age guidelines on medicines you buy or are prescribed. Sometimes people under the age of 16 need to take a lower dose than adults.

EPIPENS

Some people carry an EpiPen autoinjector to treat life-threatening allergic reactions. Doctors prescribe EpiPens to those who have a history of anaphylaxis, an allergic reaction that makes the airways swell and makes it difficult for a person to breathe. An EpiPen allows a person to inject medicine right away to counteract the allergic reaction. The person should still seek medical attention right away.

Keep Medicines Safe

Many medicines have storage instructions on the packet; read these and follow them. You may have to keep a medicine in the refrigerator or in a dark place. Many specify a temperature range for storage. They may not work if you allow them to become too hot or cold. It is also important to keep medicines safely out of reach of children. Children have small bodies that are not fully developed. Medicines that are quite safe for young adults can be very dangerous for children.

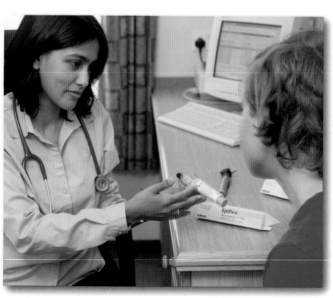

A doctor explains how to use an EpiPen to a young allergy sufferer. The drugs these pens administer can save lives in the event of an extreme allergic reaction.

A heroin addict pours out a dose of methadone, a drug designed to help with the withdrawal symptoms while coming off heroin.

Fake Drugs

Only take medicines bought from a pharmacy. Although ordering drugs online may be cheaper, it can be very dangerous. Counterfeit drugs are copies of genuine drugs, often made cheaply and without the safety controls put in place by national laws. When you buy online, you don't know whether you are getting the real thing or a copy. Often, it is impossible to tell by looking at a drug's packaging whether it is counterfeit or genuine.

Drugs vs. Drugs

Some medical drugs are used to treat people who are dependent on other drugs, such as nicotine, tobacco, and street drugs. These work in different ways. One drug treatment for alcohol, Antabuse, gives the patient an unpleasant feeling if they drink alcohol while taking the drug. Other treatments replace the drug being misused with something that produces similar effects, but in a safer way. Nicotine patches and inhalers, for example, provide nicotine without the dangers of cigarette smoke. Methadone is a replacement for heroin; it is safer to take and helps heroin addicts manage their lifestyle.

DID YOU KNOW?

Some prescription or over-the-counter drugs can be dangerous if you are pregnant, as they may pass to the unborn baby and affect its development. Even some herbal remedies may affect an unborn child. If there is any chance that you may be pregnant, you should tell your doctor or pharmacist before taking any medicines.

Medical Drugs

Even prescription drugs can be dangerous. Film star Heath Ledger died in 2008 after accidentally overdosing on prescription medicine.

When Drugs Go Wrong

Just because a drug has been prescribed does not mean that it is entirely safe. Some drugs have unpleasant side effects or can lead to further health problems. Usually, these are less unpleasant or dangerous than the original condition, and it is worth taking the drug. If you do suffer side effects, though, you should tell your doctor as there may be another drug you can use instead, or you may be able to take a lower dose. Very occasionally, people have such a bad response to a medicine they have to stop taking it.

Dependency

Not all medical drugs are safe to take for an extended period, and some medical drugs are habit forming. The tranquilizer Valium (diazepam) is an example of an addictive prescription drug. People who take it for an extended period get used to it and need an increased dose to achieve the same effect. They may also become dependent on it. If someone addicted to Valium stops taking it too suddenly, they can suffer physical withdrawal symptoms such as extreme anxiety, sleeplessness, tremors, loss of appetite, and convulsions.

FEEL-GOOD FACTOR

If you have a medical condition that persists, talk to a pharmacist or doctor rather than continuing to use over-the-counter medicines you have selected. It's easy to get it wrong if you try to diagnose your own illnesses, whereas a qualified professional can help you quickly get back to good health!

Misuse of Medical Drugs

Some nonprescription drugs can also be misused, leading to dependency or damage to health. In the United States, about 3 million people aged 12 to 25 (about 5 percent of the age group) have used over-the-counter cough and cold remedies to get high. Users can have difficulty moving and disturbed vision. These effects can last several hours. Extensive misuse of cough and cold remedies can cause lasting health problems. These drugs may not be physically addictive, but it's possible to develop a strong habit of misuse that can be hard to break.

Taking cough and cold remedies with alcohol can be especially dangerous. These remedies are often depressant drugs. As alcohol also has a depressant effect, the combination of both can, in the worst case, cause the user to fall into a coma. Taking large quantities of cold remedies can lead to extreme stomach pain, uncontrollable muscle spasms, delirium, irregular heartbeat, and even death.

Herbal and Other Remedies

Many people choose to use herbal remedies because they feel these are natural and safe. It is important to remember, though, that almost all chemicals are naturally occurring, including some of the most toxic poisons. Herbal remedies are usually not controlled in the same way as medical drugs, but they can still have an effect on your physical or mental state. Some herbal remedies are not safe when used with other drugs, including alcohol and some prescription medicines, and some should not be taken if you are pregnant.

Herbal remedies have been used for centuries—but all herbal medicines should be used with care, just like prescription drugs.

27

Performance-Enhancing Drugs

Some people turn to drugs to improve their performance in activities such as sports or school work. These are known as performance-enhancing drugs. There are several types, both legal and illegal.

Longer, Faster, Higher, Better

If you participate in sports at a regional or national level, you may come into contact with people who use drugs called anabolic steroids to improve their performance. You may even be offered them. Anabolic steroids help the body process protein and build muscle. They also help you keep going longer. If you are tempted to take steroids, bear in mind that most official sporting organizations consider using steroids to be cheating. If you get caught, you will probably be disqualified and may not even be able to train. These drugs can also damage your health. If a coach or anyone else suggests you take pills or supplements, make sure you know exactly what they are and what effect they will have on you—don't try anything you are not certain about.

FEEL-GOOD FACTOR

The healthiest way to feel your best for exams is to make sure you eat a healthy diet and get enough exercise and sleep. You can tackle nerves by using relaxation exercises instead of sedatives—these have no side effects and you can do them anywhere, at any time.

Anabolic steroids help boost muscle, but they can cause high blood pressure, high cholesterol, and damage the lungs and heart.

Cyclist Lance Armstrong leaves a drug-testing trailer. In many sports, drug testing is routine to make sure people aren't cheating.

As a stimulant, caffeine helps keep you awake and alert. Using too much, though, can make you jittery and anxious, cause sleep problems and even tremors. Caffeine increases the production of stomach acid and overuse may lead to stomach ulcers.

Even though it is legal, you can become both physically and psychologically dependent on caffeine. It is likely that many people are addicted to caffeine, though they might not notice it until they are deprived of caffeine and start to experience withdrawal symptoms. Drinking more than five cups of coffee a day may be a sign of dependence. Sudden withdrawal can cause anxiety, mood changes, muscle stiffness or pain, nausea, and headaches. These symptoms may last up to nine days.

Some young people who play a lot of sports use energy drinks to give them a boost. These contain a large amount of caffeine and other stimulants and can be habit forming.

Brain Boosters

Several companies sell dietary supplements that they claim will help boost brain power. In addition to these, some students misuse prescription drugs that are meant for people with memory problems and other mental disorders. Drugs that people take to boost their brain power include Ritalin (used for ADHD), donepezil (used to treat Alzheimer's disease), and modafinil (used to treat narcolepsy, a condition that causes people to fall asleep at odd moments). There has been little research into how these drugs affect people who are not suffering from these diseases, and they may be dangerous.

DiD YOU KNOW?

The PlayStation game Metal Gear Solid allows in-game avatars to use diazepam as an aid to keep steady while shooting. Some critics worry that this endorses the use of drugs to improve performance.

Staying Awake

To fight fatigue and get more work done before exams, some students use legal drugs such as caffeine, which can be found in coffee, tea, chocolate, cola, energy drinks, and some medicines. Caffeine is used daily by adults all over the world.

Many young people drink coffee while studying to help them stay alert, but too much caffeine in the system can affect concentration in a negative way.

Inhalant Abuse

Many everyday household substances, such as paint, glue, and aerosols, contain volatile chemicals that are easy to inhale and have intoxicating effects. Because these drugs are so readily available, it is easy for people to misuse them.

Volatile Substances

Volatile substances are those that evaporate at low temperatures and are often found in many household chemicals. Because they evaporate readily, volatile chemicals give off a vapor that can be easily inhaled. Substances that are commonly misused include glues, lighter fuels, paint and paint thinners, gasoline, and aerosols such as deodorant and hairspray.

Young people who misuse volatile substances often try them at a younger age than they would try other drugs. These substances can be found in most homes and many can be bought over the counter. Inhalant abuse can be extremely dangerous. It is difficult to control because the range of substances is wide, and it would be hard to control the sale and distribution of them all.

Effects of Inahalent Abuse

When volatile chemicals are sniffed, they enter the bloodstream rapidly and the first effects are felt after 20 to 30 seconds. The effects are similar to those of alcohol. At first, the sniffer may feel euphoric (exhilarated and happy), relaxed, and unsteady or confused. After the initial feelings wear off (in a few minutes), the sniffer often feels drowsy.

Most volatile substances are depressants. They slow down the activity of the nervous system and the brain.

REAL LIFE

"I used to inhale butane from the can, but I don't do it now. You can get like a frostbite in your mouth as the gas freezes your skin. One of my friends nearly suffocated. He blacked out with the can still in his mouth. It just kept going, freezing his throat."

Kieran, 17

These substances also can act as stimulants, though. They can make you feel sick, disoriented, confused, and aggressive. They can make you vomit, give you headaches, make you wheeze, or cause blackouts. If you pass out and vomit, you can suffocate. Hallucinations, mood swings, and terrifying, unreasonable fears are some of the psychological side effects of continued misuse.

Dangers of Death

It is not uncommon for volatile substances to have extreme, unpleasant, and even fatal effects. This can happen the very first time a person sniffs volatile substances or on any later occasion. Approximately one-quarter of deaths from volatile substances occur on first use. The most dangerous effects include heart attacks, suffocation, or accidents caused by being reckless or uncoordinated.

Volatile substances can make your heart beat irregularly. If you then put extra stress on your heart, through exertion, fear, or excitement, your heart may be unable to cope, resulting in a heart attack.

Over a period of time, misuse of solvents can destroy brain cells, leading to brain damage. It can affect your kidneys, sight, hearing, lungs, and liver.

Some users inhale butane gas straight from the can into their mouth.

Approximately 100 substances are regularly used for sniffing—about 30 are common in many households.

DID YOU KNOW?

Inhalant abuse causes more deaths among people ages 10 to 16 than all controlled drugs put together. As many people between the ages of 25 to 35 die of solvent abuse as do young people under 25.

Inhalant Abuse

Inhalant abuse such as sniffing glue, can be extremely dangerous and carries risks of suffocation or heart attack.

Suffocation

Some users put a bag over their head to keep the vapor near their nose and mouth. This is very dangerous. If you pass out with a bag over your head, or a gas bottle hissing into your mouth, you can easily suffocate. If you breathe in too much of a volatile substance, your blood will not be able to carry enough oxygen to your organs. This can cause organ failure, leading to serious illness or death. More than 2 million U.S. teens have used inhalants to get high. Approximately 100 teens die each year from inhaling volatile substances.

Accidents Happen

Just like someone intoxicated with alcohol, those who have misused volatile substances have impaired judgement. They may take risks they would never take under normal circumstances. In addition to the dangerous direct effects on the body, there is a real danger of being in an accident, falling from a high building or wall, or falling into water and drowning. Volatile substances are usually flammable. If you use them while smoking, or around people who are smoking, there is a danger of setting fire to the gases from the substance and being burned or causing a fire.

Warning Signs

Signs of inhalant abuse include:

- unusual breath odor
- chemical odor on clothing
- slurred or slowed speech
- paint products on face or fingers
- hidden aerosol paint cans
- chemical odor on clothing
- lack of coordination
- inattentiveness
- unable to see clearly

Dependence

Volatile substances are not physically addictive, but some people develop a psychological dependence on them which can be difficult to break. Many people who go on to use other drugs—whether legal or illegal—first misused volatile substances. The majority of illegal drug users have misused volatile substances at some point.

DID YOU KNOW?

In the mid-1990s, approximately one in five U.S. teens got high by using inhalants. According to the National Institute on Drug Abuse (NIDA), many became "hooked" in elementary school.

Crime rates are high among young people who misuse volatile substances because they often take risks when they are high.

FEEL-GOOD FACTOR

Only use volatile chemicals in a well-ventilated area. For instance, don't paint a room with the windows and doors closed. Take frequent breaths outside in the fresh air if you are using volatile substances for more than a few minutes.

GASOLINE SNIFFING

In Australia, gasoline sniffing is especially common among aboriginal populations with high levels of unemployment and poverty. To combat the dangers, Australia has introduced a new gasoline that has a greatly reduced effect when sniffed. Gasoline sniffing has been cut to one-sixth of previous rates.

Party Drugs

Many people use drugs on weekends when they go to concerts or dance parties. They use the drugs to help them relax and because they feel the drugs enhance the music or dancing. But party drugs can have dangerous effects on the body and mind.

Designs on ecstasy tablets include hearts, rabbits, mushrooms, and champagne bottles.

Ecstasy—The Happy Drug

Ecstasy is sold as pills. It gives users a buzz that makes them feel happy and in tune with their surroundings and friends. Ecstasy helps people stay awake longer than they could without the drug. It takes about 30 minutes for Ecstasy to take effect, and the buzz lasts between three and six hours. However, there is a danger of taking too much. Some people take a second dose because the first does doesn't seem to work, and then both doses take effect.

The long-term effects of taking Ecstasy are not yet known for certain. There may be a link with depression, memory loss, and personality change. Although many people take Ecstasy with no obvious ill-effects, there are occasional deaths as a result of Ecstasy use, sometimes after the first use of a single tablet.

Sex, Drugs, and Rock 'n' Roll?

Many of the drugs people use recreationally at music festivals, clubs, raves, and parties are common in lots of other situations, too. Alcohol, tobacco, and marijuana are the most widely used. But there are also drugs that are associated more closely with the music and dance scene and are used less often elsewhere. These include Ecstasy (E), ketamine (K), magic mushrooms, poppers, and speed.

ECSTASY PILLS

Ecstasy is supplied as tablets in many different colors, often stamped with a design (such as a smiley face or a heart). Unlike many other drugs, most of which come from plants, Ecstasy is an artificial drug, produced in laboratories from chemical ingredients.

Some people, particularly those with asthma, epilepsy, or a heart condition, may have a very dangerous reaction to Ecstasy.

Ecstasy is not physically addictive, but some people develop a tolerance and take increased amounts to get the same effect. It is also possible to form a psychological habit and feel the drug is necessary in order to have a good time. Sometimes, Ecstasy is cut (mixed) with other substances, such as caffeine or speed, which may change the effects it has or make the effects stronger.

Ketamine is often illegally supplied as a powder for snorting.

Ketamine

Ketamine, or K, is a strong drug that causes hallucinations and a temporary loss of feeling. It may make you feel that your body and mind have been separated. Medical ketamine is injected as a liquid. Sometimes tablets of ketamine are passed off as Ecstasy.

Ketamine is not physically addictive, but may cause psychological dependence. If you take ketamine regularly, your body can become used to it so you need a larger dose to achieve the same effect. Ketamine can cause panic attacks, depression, and anxiety. Large doses can be dangerous, particularly if taken with alcohol, as they can slow the heart rate and breathing to the point where you may become unconscious. Because of its anaesthetic effects, you cannot feel pain if you have taken ketamine, so there is a chance that you may injure yourself badly and not seek medical help. Deaths related to ketamine use are usually the result of accidents.

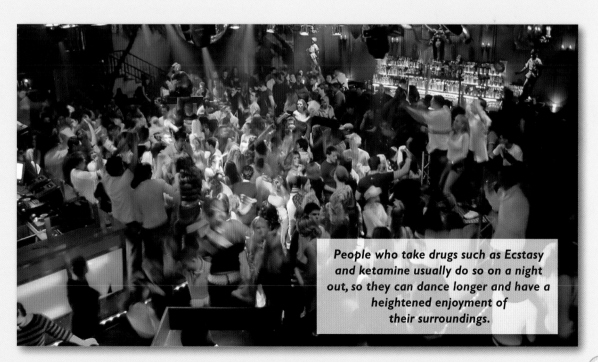

People who take drugs such as Ecstasy and ketamine usually do so on a night out, so they can dance longer and have a heightened enjoyment of their surroundings.

Party Drugs

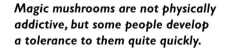

Magic mushrooms are not physically addictive, but some people develop a tolerance to them quite quickly.

terrifying hallucinations or are unable to deal with synesthesia. It is possible to have flashbacks to a "bad trip" for some time after the effects of the mushrooms have worn off. If you have mental health problems, magic mushrooms may worsen them. You may lose track of time, which might seem to pass very quickly or dreadfully slowly.

Poppers

Poppers are small bottles of a liquid chemical called amyl nitrite. Sniffed straight from the bottle, it produces an intense, but short-lived, high. The effect wears off in about two minutes. Using poppers may give you a headache or a rash around the mouth. Poppers are highly flammable, so smoking while using poppers is dangerous. They also are deadly poisonous if swallowed. They can burn you if they come into contact with skin and can be especially dangerous for people with heart conditions, chest problems, or the eye disease glaucoma.

Magic Mushrooms

Magic mushrooms are a type of fungus that grows wild in forests in some areas. Eating them raw can make a person sick, so most people cook them first. Magic mushrooms cause hallucinations. The "trip" usually starts between 30 minutes and two hours after eating them. The main part of the "trip" lasts between four and ten hours. After-effects last an additional two to six hours. During this period, you may feel confident, happy, and relaxed. You may also feel that your senses are jumbled up—that you can hear colors or see sounds. This effect is called synesthesia.

One of the dangers of magic mushrooms is having a "bad trip." Some people have

DID YOU KNOW?

Some toadstools are very poisonous. People suffer ill effects every year after eating toadstools that they believed were edible or hallucinogenic mushrooms. Don't eat mushrooms you have found.

Poppers, or amyl nitrite, are most commonly used in nightclubs and gay bars.

Poppers do not cause physical or psychological dependence and have been used safely as medicine for the heart condition angina for many years.

Speed

Speed, or amphetamine, is a powerful stimulant. Some people take it when they go clubbing because it enables them to dance all night without getting tired. The effects can be felt about half an hour after taking speed and last four to six hours. There is a long come-down period, which can last a day or two.

Speed may be supplied as a powder or crystals, which is rubbed on the gums, snorted, or swallowed. Prescription amphetamines are used to treat illnesses such as ADHD and come in the form of pills. Crystal meth is a very strong and highly addictive form of speed.

Speed causes physical dependency. Increased doses are needed to get the same effect as the body builds up tolerance to it. The main dangers of speed use, apart from addiction, are symptoms such as depression, anxiety, and aggression. Taking speed with antidepressants or alcohol can be deadly. Taking a lot, especially over a few days, can cause panic and paranoia. This usually subsides once the drug leaves the body.

KNOW WHAT YOU'RE TAKING

Some people take any pills they are offered, which can be very dangerous. If you have no idea what is in a drug or what it could do to you, taking it may put you at risk of death. Mixing unknown drugs or pills and alcohol can produce a lethal cocktail.

Street Drugs

All drugs—including party drugs—that are illicitly produced and illegally supplied can be termed street drugs. However, some are more commonly associated with addiction, dependency, and social problems. These include heroin, crack cocaine, and crystal meth.

Heroin

Heroin is a painkiller, often misused as a depressant. The immediate effect of a small dose is a quick rush or buzz often followed by a feeling of warmth and well-being. Larger doses can make users sleepy and relaxed. People are sometimes dizzy and sick when they first use heroin. It is a highly addictive drug, but the body builds up tolerance to it. Increased doses are needed to get an effect or, after a while, just to feel normal.

There is a prolonged come down period after taking heroin and severe or unpleasant withdrawal symptoms for a user who gives up too suddenly. Some users spend $50 to $100

FEEL-GOOD FACTOR

There are safer alternatives to heroin that produce a comparable effect in the body, such as methadone and Subutex. These are available on prescription to users who want to stop taking the illegal drug and lead a more stable life. Naltrexone can block the effects of heroin to dissuade ex-users from returning to the drug.

Drugs such as heroin are often bought illegally from dealers on the street.

a day on heroin, desperate to avoid the symptoms that come with not taking it.

On the street, heroin is sold as a powder, ranging in color from white to brown. Supplied in small bags, the heroin is mixed with other substances. These can be flour, sugar, powdered milk, or quinine. Occasionally, more harmful substances are used, including nutmeg and brick dust. The average purity of street heroin in the United States is 35 percent —which means that 65 percent of it is other substances that can be extremely harmful. It is also available as bricks of dark-colored resin.

Coke users cut the powder to make it fine, often using the edge of a credit card, and then snort it through a straw or a rolled-up dollar bill.

has lost its tolerance and they take too much. Accidental overdoses also occur if someone takes an unusually pure sample, which delivers more heroin than expected. The most common risks from heroin misuse are related to using dirty needles. Diseases such as HIV/AIDS and hepatitis can be carried by shared needles; septicaemia and gangrene can result from infections caused by dirty needles.

Cocaine and Crack Cocaine

Cocaine is a powerful stimulant with a short-lived effect. After taking cocaine, people feel confident, buzzy, and full of energy. It also raises the heart rate and body temperature. Cocaine is supplied as a white powder that is snorted, but there are two variants, freebase and crack, which usually are smoked. Crack comes in the form of small rocks that crack as they burn. Smoking crack or freebase produces a more rapid effect than snorting. Both powdered cocaine and crack can be dissolved and injected.

Overdosing

There are many health risks associated with heroin use, including a considerable risk of death from overdosing. Death from a heroin overdose is most common when it is used with other drugs, including alcohol. The combined effects of depressant drugs can stop a person from breathing and slow the heartbeat, leading to coma or death. People who have been heroin-free for a time sometimes overdose if they take the drug again, as their body

REAL LIFE

"I worked in an office where people had to work all night to meet deadlines in a really stressful situation. After about 2 A.M., they'd snort cocaine from the flat-screen monitors. They'd lay them on the desk and do a line of coke to get through the next hour's work. The problem was, they were then too buzzed and distracted to really get the work done."
Paulina, 17

Street Drugs

This drug user is getting rid of his old needles as part of a needle-exchange program, which helps limit the spread of disease from dirty needles.

The Effects of Cocaine

The effect of cocaine takes about two minutes to peak if it is smoked as crack, longer if it is snorted. Many users feel tempted to take more immediately because of the short-lived effect. After using cocaine, people often have flu-like symptoms and low moods, sometimes a few days after taking the drug. Psychological dependence is usually more of a problem than the physical effects of withdrawal, but cocaine is a habit-forming drug and difficult to give up. Extended use of cocaine can make people appear nervous and jittery with paranoid fantasies that others are out to get them or cause them harm. If they stop using cocaine, these side effects disappear.

INJECTING DRUGS

Injecting repeatedly can damage blood vessels to the point where they can no longer be pierced by a needle. Repeated injections (not in a medical setting) can also lead to tissue damage and gangrene. In extreme cases, it can result in the loss of limbs.

LSD is supplied on paper or in sugar cubes impregnated with the drug. It can take 20 minutes to two hours for the acid to take effect after swallowing the paper or sugar cube.

Mixing Cocaine and Heroin

Some cocaine users start taking heroin to dull their craving for cocaine and, as a result, become dependent on heroin. Speedballing is injecting a mixture of cocaine and heroin. This is very dangerous: famous figures thought to have died from speedballing include actors River Phoenix and John Belushi, as well as the artist Jean-Michel Basquiat.

LSD

LSD, or acid, could be classified as a dance or party drug, as some people take it at concerts or when they go clubbing. It is dangerous to take it on a night out, though, as the extreme hallucinogenic effects can make it impossible to get home safely. LSD causes "trips" lasting up to 12 hours. Users often see the world transformed into swirling colors or have bizarre visions, such as very strange and vivid dreams. A "bad trip" can be a terrifying experience, though, and may haunt someone for months or even years in the form of vivid flashbacks. Some people harm themselves, either accidentally or in an attempt to get out of a "bad trip." There is no way of knowing whether the drug will cause a good or bad experience—and no way out after taking the LSD.

People who have mental health problems may be in danger of making it worse or having a "bad trip" if they take LSD. Taking it while feeling down or depressed, even without underlying mental health problems, can still lead to a "bad trip."

REAL LIFE

"After taking LSD, I went in the elevator, but thought it was on fire because of the little red light. When it got to the ground floor I was screaming. I saw my face reflected in the metal. My skin was all melting off revealing my skull, and my eyes were just in deep pits. I started to scream again." Kerry, 17

Street Drugs

Meth

Methamphetamine is a powerful stimulant that comes in different forms—powder, pills, or crystals. The powder or pills can be swallowed or they can be dissolved and injected. The crystal or ice form (crystal meth) is smoked in a pipe. This takes effect more quickly than other ways of taking the drug. Meth gives people a rush of energy, suppresses appetite, creates a feeling of euphoria, and increases sexual activity. It can also produce hyperthermia, increased heart rate and blood pressure, confusion, aggression, psychosis, and convulsions. Hyperthermia and convulsions can be fatal. An overdose can lead to a stroke, damage to organs, a coma, and death. Regular use of meth causes physical and psychological dependency. As users become more tolerant of the drug, they may increase their intake to achieve the same effects. Withdrawal symptoms can include depression and anxiety.

These young men are smoking crystal meth. They are addicted to the drug, but say it makes them feel invincible.

Why Take Them?

Most street drugs are illegal and can be very dangerous—so why do people take them? Some try them out of curiosity or a sense of adventure. Many drugs—both legal and illegal—have a social aspect, and people often try them in a social setting where friends are taking them. This is particularly true of party or dance drugs, such as Ecstasy, and of alcohol, tobacco, and marijuana. Some people turn to drugs because they hope drugs will help them to cope with emotional pain, trauma, or problems in their lives. They hope to forget and want the oblivion that drugs offer. Taking drugs in this frame of mind is more dangerous than taking them when you are feeling happy and is more likely to lead to misuse, recklessness, and dependency.

DID YOU KNOW?

Almost half of all new HIV/AIDS cases in the United States are related to use of crystal meth, which removes inhibitions that lead people to have unprotected sex, sometimes with strangers.

Drugs and Your Body

Some of the drugs discussed in this chapter are associated with typical images of junkies—often run-down, terribly thin addicts who may be on the verge of death. That picture is one of an extreme case of drug dependency. Not all heroin, crack, or crystal meth users will end up like that. For many users, though, health problems are brought on by the change in lifestyle that drug misuse or dependency often brings. People may stop eating properly (stimulant drugs suppress appetite); they may not sleep well, may exercise very little, or let their standards of hygiene slip. With an immune system weakened by these habits, drug users are vulnerable to minor and more serious illnesses.

Staying Healthy

Your body has not developed to deal with an overload of substances that affect your physical or mental state. While it may be able to process some of them in moderate doses, overdoing any kind of drug puts you at risk—even prescription drugs may have side effects that have to be balanced against the benefits they bring. It is best not to use drugs at all, but if you do choose to use alcohol or another nonmedical drug, stick to moderate, controlled use, and make sure that you eat a healthy diet and exercise.

Coming Off Drugs

There is a lot of help available to anyone who wants to quit drugs. Trying to persuade someone to quit when they don't want to is very difficult, if not impossible. How difficult it is to quit depends on the individual, the drug they are using, their motivation to quit, and the level of physical or psychological dependency they have developed. The benefits of quitting start to show immediately.

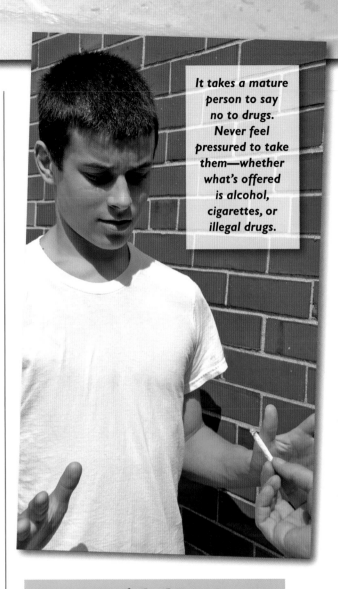

It takes a mature person to say no to drugs. Never feel pressured to take them—whether what's offered is alcohol, cigarettes, or illegal drugs.

REAL LIFE

"I started smoking when I was seven and went on to more and more drugs as my life fell apart. My stepfather beat me, I was bullied at school—it all got out of control. I was busted for dealing when I was 16. My drug counselor turned things around for me. After prison, I started training as a counselor myself." Matthew, 20

Glossary

adrenalin a natural stimulant produced by the body; it can be injected to combat serious allergic reactions

anabolic steroid a drug used by some athletes to improve stamina and build muscle, related to the human hormone testosterone

attention-deficit hyperactivity disorder (ADHD) a disorder that leads children to have a short attention span and behave boisterously

black market illegal trade carried on outside the normal commercial environment, which avoids controls and taxation

bronchitis an inflammation of the airways in the lungs, often caused by inhaling smoke, dust, or fumes

caffeine a stimulant that occurs naturally in coffee, tea, chocolate, and some other foods and drinks

carbon monoxide a gas that causes poisoning by preventing the blood from carrying oxygen

chemotherapy a medical treatment that uses powerful chemicals to kill microorganisms (such as bacteria) or cancer cells

convulsion involuntary movement of the muscles, causing the body to twitch and jerk uncontrollably

delirium an inability to focus attention, sometimes linked with disorientation, hallucinations, or stupor

diabetes a condition in which the body does not produce insulin and is unable to regulate the amount of sugar in the blood

emphysema a serious lung condition caused by inhaling irritants such as cigarette smoke, leading to severe breathing difficulties

epilepsy a condition that causes a person to have seizures

gangrene a condition in which body tissue dies and rots away

hallucination a vivid and often bizarre perception of something that is not real

hemophilia a medical condition in which the blood does not clot, even a minor wound will bleed for a very long time

hepatitis an inflammation of the liver caused by disease or poisoning (including alcohol poisoning)

hyperthermia a condition in which the body overheats and is unable to cool itself down

metabolize the ability of the body to deal with chemicals coming into the body, using them for nutrition or respiration or getting rid of them

nicotine a harmful and habit-forming chemical found in tobacco

psychological relating to mental disorders

schizophrenia a mental disorder characterized by abnormal perception of reality, including hallucinations, unreasonable fears, delusions, and strange, irrational behavior

sedative a drug that has a calming effect

septicemia a bacterial infection of the blood, leading to severe illness affecting the whole body

skunk a strong form of marijuana

spirit a strong, distilled alcoholic drink, such as gin or vodka

stimulant a chemical that increases alertness and awareness

stoned intoxicated by the use of marijuana.

tranquilizer a drug that has a calming effect

Further Information

Books

Drowning in a Bottle: Teens and Alcohol Abuse
by Gail B. Stewart
(Compass Point Books, 2009)

Drugs: The Real Deal
by Rachel Lynette
(Heinemann Library, 2008)

How to Say No and Keep Your Friends
by Sharon Scott
(Human Resource Development, 1997)

Living with Alcoholism and Addiction
by Nicholas R. Lessa
(Checkmark Books, 2009)

Prescription Drug Abuse (What's the Deal?)
by Karla Fitzhugh
(Heinemann Library, 2006)

Straight Talking series
by Sean Conolly
(Smart Apple Media, 2007)

Teenagers and Tobacco: Nicotine and the Adolescent Brain
by Katie John Sharp
(Mason Crest Publishers, 2009)

Voices: Drugs on the Street
by Anne Rooney
(Smart Apple Media, 2007)

Web Sites

http://kidshealth.org/teen/drug_alcohol/ tobacco/smoking.html
This site for teens explains how smoking affects the body, how to kick the habit, and stay smoke free.

http://www.streetdrugs.org
Unbiased facts about drug use and misuse.

http://teens.drugabuse.gov/facts/index.php
Learn how different drugs impact the brain and body.

http://familydoctor.org/online/famdocen/ home/children/teens.html
This site offers information on drugs, smoking, alcohol, peer pressure, and more.

http://teenshealth.org/teen/drug_alcohol/
Facts about how alcohol and drugs affect your body and health.

http://teens.drugabuse.gov/facts/facts_ ster1.php
This site explains the affects of anabolic steroids to the mind and body

Index